Start Up Easy Guide Vol. 3

Choosing a business location and negotiating a lease

Start Up Easy Guide

Life Solutions Publishing, LLC
PO Box 1411
Fairburn GA 30213

ISBN-13: 978-1500805104
ISBN-10: 1500805106

Note to the Reader

This book is for informational purposes only. The author has endeavored to make sure it contains helpful information. However, city, state, and local laws change frequently, as well as, leasing policies. It is the reader's responsibility to search matters pertaining to their particular business. The author nor the publisher is assuming the role of a professional business advisor. Before adopting any suggestions made in this book, it is recommended that the reader do further research. Individual readers are solely responsible for their own business decisions, and the author and the publisher do not accept responsibility for any adverse effects individuals or businesses may claim to experience, whether directly or indirectly, based on information contained herein.

Contents

Introduction

I want to congratulate you for becoming an owner of this book. In doing so, you have just gotten one step closer to becoming a business owner. The "Start Up Easy Guide" series was designed with people like you in mind. The goal of each book in the series is to equip you with the knowledge you need to make the startup of your business easy. In this volume, you will learn important tips and steps to take for the critical decision of choosing a business location. Every year there are business failures and there are many reasons for the failures; choosing the wrong business location is often at the top of the list.

The goal of this book is to help you make decisions that will lead to your success. We hope to help you achieve that success by drawing from many years of knowledge and the experiences of business owners. Remember, success doesn't just happen, it is planned for. Our wish is for you to have the greatest success in your business endeavors. Best wishes – Life Solutions.

Chapter 1
Demographics

When choosing a location for your business, always research the areas demographics.

Demographics = *Statistical Data Relating To The Population And Particular Groups Within It.*

Whether leasing or purchasing you must know the demographics in and around the area where you plan to locate your business. Depending on the type of business you're opening, the study of demographics can be critical to your success or failure. If you are opening a business that will depend on the selling of a product or service to people in a particular region or area, the study of demographics is a must. Most shopping center leasing agents can provide you with this information quickly and easily.

If you have heeded the suggestions given in "Start Up Easy Guide" Volume 1, you should have already identified your potential customers by age, gender, family status, and income level. And now that you have this information about your potential customers, you must use demographics to find a location that will allow you to reach the people most likely to purchase your product or service. If you don't know who your customers are you will never know if a location will be a good fit for your business. Before opening a martial arts school there was a business owner that did research to find out the average income levels of families and the average ages of students that were taking martial arts lessons. He discovered that in order for him to have a successful school he needed to attract families with high levels of disposable income and that a majority of martial arts students were elementary school-aged children.

Knowing the statistics from his particular industry allowed him to select a location that was close to elementary schools that contained families with high disposable income. Remember, success doesn't just happen; it must be planned for. It doesn't matter how great your product or service is, if you choose the wrong business location, no one will ever know about it. You must ask yourself if the customers that will value and be willing to purchase your product or service are in and around the location you're thinking of choosing; are they there in large enough numbers to sustain your business, and can they afford it. If you're in a business that will not be driven by local statistics, you must ask yourself if that location is ideal for shipping and receiving or reaching your target customers in other ways.

Traffic Count = A traffic count is a count of traffic along a particular road.

If your business will depend upon or be helped by large numbers of people moving in and out of the area of your business location, you are going to want to be sure that you know the locations traffic count. Knowing the traffic count of a particular location will give you a great deal of important information. For instance, knowing an areas traffic count will tell you exactly how many people may or may not see your business sign and how many potential customers you could have or gain by choosing the location. We feel pretty comfortable giving you a guarantee that most of the gas stations located on highway exits have a really good idea of what that highway's traffic count is. Remember, success doesn't just happen, it is planned for through research.

Demographics

☐ Identify your target customers by age, income level, and family status.

☐ Obtain demographics for your potential location from a commercial realtor or research firm.

Using what you know about your target customers,

☐ Examine the demographics to determine whether or not the potential location will be a good match for your business.

Ask yourself the following questions:

☐ What percentage of the residents in this area are in my targeted income group?

☐ Are the number of residents that are in my targeted income group large enough for me to have a sustainable customer base?

☐ What are the growth projections for this area for the next 10 years?

☐ Are the growth projections for the area high enough to potentially grow my business long term?

☐ What is the location's traffic count and how will it affect my business?

Chapter 2
Current Tenants

Before contacting anyone about a potential location, we recommend talking to current tenants to find out what type of landlord you would potentially have. If they are happy, chances are, you will be happy. Here are a few questions that you may want to ask the current tenants:

Ask: How long have you been at this location?

Someone that's a new tenant will not be a great source of information.

Ask: How quick is management to respond to maintenance or repair issues?

If the air conditioning goes out in your unit in the middle of August and management takes two weeks to fix it, you could be out of a lot of money. No matter how good your product or service is or how loyal your customers are, people are not likely to spend much time in your business if they'll need a shower after leaving.

Ask: What do you think of the area?

Local business owners are the first to notice new trends in the area.

Ask: What is the average costs to lease here?

An honest answer to this question could potentially keep you from overpaying. This question will be best answered by someone who has been in their lease for under three years as prices may have been a lot cheaper for tenants that have been located there longer. Try not to offend anyone by directly asking them what they're paying each month. Remember, this is a potential neighbor and you want the relationship to start off on the right foot.

Chapter 2 Check List
Current Tenants

☐ Ask how long they have been at the location.

☐ Ask if they and the other tenants have a good relationship with the management/landlord.

☐ Ask how quick is management to respond to maintenance or repair issues.

☐ Ask what they think of the area.

☐ Ask about the average cost to lease. (Remember DO NOT ask them how much they are paying).

☐ Ask if they would recommend that you locate your business there.

Chapter 3
Parking

In order for your business to be successful your customers must have access to your products or services. When choosing a location, parking is a very important consideration. Your location must have parking that adequately matches your particular business. The martial arts school owner that was mentioned earlier, knew and understood that parking would be critical to his business. He not only had to think about a location with enough spaces for parents to park, but he had to make sure it was safe for small children to enter and exit the location after parking.

He estimated that on average, there would be at least 20 non-related students in class. This meant that at any given time, there needed to be at least 20 parking spaces available for his customers; not to mention, the occasional visit from grandpa, grandma, and other relatives. The school owner used this information to determine that he needed a location that would have at least 20 available parking spaces for his customers. Your particular business may not need 20 parking spaces, but you must know and take time to think about how many spaces your operation will require. When calculating parking, you must also know the peak hours of your business.

If you're running a sandwich shop that is located near several office parks, then you need to know how much parking is available between the hours of 11am and 1pm; no one wants to spend half of their lunch hour searching for somewhere to park. Remember, people cannot and will not buy your products or services if they can't find a place to park. When choosing a business location, parking MUST be one of the things you consider.

Chapter 3 Check List
Parking

☐ Estimate the amount of customers you expect to have each day.

☐ Determine your business peak hours of the day and busiest days of the week.

☐ Find out if there are a certain number of parking spaces allocated to each tenant.

☐ Ask other tenants if they feel that the location has adequate parking.

☐ Visit the location during your peak hours and days of the week and count the amount of empty spaces during those times to determine if your customers would have adequate parking.

☐ Know the peak hours of businesses that will be located next to you and around you.

☐ Use a separate checklist for each potential location so that you may compare pros and cons.

Chapter 4
Lighting

If your business will be open after dark, the lighting in a potential business location is something that must be considered. Lighting is important for your business and your ability to attract customers. Customers normally won't flock to a location known as the "black hole." Your location or center must be well lit at all times. Well lit locations will be attractive places for customers such as women, women with children, and men with families. A lack of lighting can cost your business dearly if you are planning to keep later hours.

Remember, darkness is often a cover for criminals seeking to make victims out of you or your customers. You also don't want to be known as the business where people fall and hurt themselves outside of your door because poor lighting. Good lighting is a must for later hours. Drive by the potential location from both directions to determine whether or not the business can be easily seen from the street at night. If the location is hard for you to see at night, chances are, it will be hard for your customers to see also. Remember, you will not make money if your business cannot be seen. If a location's lighting is not well maintained, it may not be worth moving to that location.

Chapter 4 Check List
Lighting

☐ Determine whether or not your business will be open after dark.

☐ Visit potential locations after dark to determine the amount of lighting your business will have.

☐ Drive by the location from both directions to determine whether or not the business can be easily seen from the street at night.

☐ Do an injury risk assessment of the potential location based on the amount of lighting. (Ask yourself if the amount of lighting would put your potential customers at high risk for falls or other injuries).

☐ Do a crime risk assessment of the potential location based on the amount of lighting. (Ask yourself if the amount of lighting would attract criminals and make it easy for crimes to be committed under the cover of darkness. Ask yourself if you were a criminal, would you view the location is an easy target).

Chapter 5
Crime

In addition to lighting, there's another factor that needs to be considered where safety is concerned. That factor is crime. When considering a location, do some research to find out if the location is safe. We are often surprised when we hear people say that an area *feels* safe. *Feelings* are okay for an individual, but not for a business owner who is potentially about to invest their life savings into a location. In business, feelings aren't enough; you must do your homework. The answer to the questions that you need can normally be found at the local Police Department. Here are a few questions that you should ask:

Ask: *How many crimes have taken place at that location within the last five years?*

Ask: *Are the number of crimes in the area trending upward or downward?*

This will give you a general idea of whether or not the area is safe and a potentially good location for your business.

Ask: *How many of the recent crimes in the area have been violent crimes?*
This will tell you if the area is dealing with a few disorderly youths or hardened criminals.

Ask: *If the police patrol the area and if so, how often.*
A strong police presence is always a deterrent to crime.

Chapter 5 Check List
Crime

☐ Ask current business owners in the area and at the location if a crime has ever been committed in or around their business.

☐ Ask the local police how many crimes have taken place at the location within the last five years.

☐ Ask if the number of crimes in the area are trending upward or downward.

☐ Ask how many of the recent crimes in the area have been violent crimes.

☐ Ask if the police patrol the area and if so, how often.

Chapter 6
Zoning

When considering a location, you must always ask if the area is zoned for the type of business you wish to operate.

Zoning= The separation or division of a municipality into districts, the regulation of buildings and structures in such districts in accordance with their construction and the nature and extent of their use, and the dedication of such districts to particular uses designed to serve the general welfare.

The three most common types of zones are residential, commercial, and industrial. Local governments often use zoning in an effort to protect the quality of life of their citizens and the property values of real estate. Most people would not be willing to purchase a home next to a lot that could become a Land Field. Zoning gives confidence to citizens that their property values will be protected by restricting building projects and uses that could potentially threaten the value of their property. Zoning also gives city planners the tools they need to prevent overbuilding and overcrowding, and to be sure that streets and roads are able to handle the type of traffic and vehicles that will be using them. It is important to keep in mind that within each type of zoning area there may also be different levels of densities that are allowed.

Density= Degree to which something is filled, crowded, or occupied; the number of individuals, such as inhabitants or housing units, per unit of area.

For example, if a developer wanted to build a subdivision, they would most likely purchase land that is located in a low density residential zone. If that same developer wanted to build townhomes, they would probably seek out a medium density residential zone. And if they wanted to build a 30 story condominium high-rise, they would purchase land in a high density residential zone. You should also be aware that within commercial and industrial zones there are sometimes specific restrictions for certain industries. It is important to do your homework and to understand zoning laws in your area. Depending on the type and size of your business, zoning could be a very important factor for you to consider when choosing a location.

Knowledge of an area's zoning laws could also be the key to making serious profits. For example, if 100 acres of land had suddenly been zoned as high density residential, the newly zoned area might be a great place to locate your business because of the potential number of customers. With the right information, an area's zoning can work to your advantage and help you create an extremely successful business.

Chapter 6 Check List
Zoning

☐ Ask if the potential location is zoned for the type of business you wish to operate.

☐ Find out whether or not the zoning density will be a good match for the size of your business.

☐ Research whether or not there are local or state requirements for your specific type of business.

☐ Find out if there have been any recent zoning changes in and around the areas of your potential location. (This may work to your business advantage or disadvantage).

Chapter 7
How long?

As you consider selecting a location for your new business, there are two questions that you should ask; how long do you want to commit to a particular location? And if you're renting, what are the terms of the lease? In order to answer the question of how long you want to commit to a particular location, you must know the answer to this question, "Who are your customers?" If your customers are the type who will potentially move around a lot, purchasing a location or signing a long-term lease should not be an option for you. However, if your customers are going to be long-term residents of a particular area (homeowners instead of renters) then the longer your commitment, the better it will be for your business.

Keep in mind that there are often financial benefits to long-term commitments. Landlords are usually willing to throw in more incentives and cheaper rent prices to tenants that are willing to commit to longer leases. In order to make the right decision, you must not only know who your customers are, you must also know what their future actions may be. For instance, if your business is located near a military base that is being considered for closure within the next few years, you must consider this when deciding whether to buy a location or how long to lease a location and what type of clauses should be included in the lease. If hundreds of your customers could potentially move away, then you must have the flexibility in your lease to move along with them. This can be accomplished by simply adding an amendment to the lease that gives you the freedom to cancel it at the end of every one-year period.

If your customers are homeowners in a city that is projected to continue growing and several new subdivisions will be built over the next few years, it may be best for you to purchase a location or commit to a long-term lease of five years or more. Keep in mind, you must not commit to a location beyond its proven ability to provide your business with customers.

Chapter 7 Check List
How Long?

☐ Based on growth projections, determine how long you will feel comfortable committing to that particular location.

☐ If leasing, find out the minimum term of the lease.

☐ Ask about the lease renewal rates that will apply after the initial lease period. You will need these numbers for long-term budget projections.

☐ If comfortable with the area and your research about its future, inquire about incentives for signing a longer-term lease.

☐ If uncomfortable about the locations future, be sure to ask about a buyout or early cancellation amendment.

Chapter 8
How Much?

There are four things to consider when trying to determine how much a particular location will cost you each month; CAM and utilities, which we will discuss later, costs per square foot and yearly increases. As you go around to different centers and call to inquire about costs, you will most often receive an answer that involves the amount per square foot. These prices can vary and can be expensive or cheap depending on the amount of space you wish to lease. The only way to know the true costs is to know how to calculate the dollar amount per square foot by the amount of space you wish to lease. Here is a simple formula for calculating monthly rent based on cost per square foot.

- Determining Monthly Cost by Square Footage.

To determine the total square footage of a space take the length of a space in feet and the width of a space in feet and multiply the two numbers by each other and this will give you the total square footage.

For example:

If a space is 40 X 60 feet the total square footage would equal 2400 square feet.

If the price is set at $15 per square foot, then the monthly cost could be calculated like this:

$15 per sq ft x 2400 square feet = $36,000 annually divided by 12 months = $3,000.

Using this formula, you can calculate that a 2400 sq ft space at $15 per square foot would cost you $3000 per month.

The formula to use is:

Cost per sq ft x the amount of space for lease = Annual rent, divided by 12 months = Monthly Rent.

- Find out if the lease will be an escalating lease? (Will rent increase each year?)

Once you have determined the monthly cost of your lease, the next question you should ask is if the lease will be an escalating lease; in other words, will the cost of the lease increase each year. In some centers, rent will increase with the projected growth of your business. It is important, for budgeting purposes, to know what your operating costs will be each year. Be sure to ask about renewal rates beyond the initial lease period - (sometimes rental rates can jump sharply at the time of renewal).

Never assume that cost will remain the same, always have a long-term plan; this will help you determine if leasing at that particular center will allow you to meet your long-term profit goals. Remember, your goal is to make a profit for yourself, not the landlord.

Chapter 8 Check List
How Much?

☐ When inquiring about the costs of a particular location, always ask if there are CAM (Common Area Maintenance) charges.

☐ If CAM charges are a part of the lease, find out if the lease will require you to pay a set CAM amount or if charges will be paid as a percentage.

☐ When receiving quotes in costs of square footage, remember to use the following formula: *Cost per Sq ft x the Amount of space for lease = Annual rent, Divided by 12 months = Monthly Rent Cost.*

☐ Compare the cost per square foot with other locations you might be considering to determine the best deal.

☐ Ask if utilities are included in monthly rent charges.

Chapter 9
Leasing Incentives

- Free or Reduced Rent

If a center really wants you and your business as a tenant, they will often offer leasing incentives. One of the most common incentives is free or reduced rent at the beginning of the lease to help you with the cost of move in and setup. It's important to know that this is a pretty common practice and that even if it is not offered, you shouldn't hesitate to ask for it. Receiving 1 to 3 free or reduced months at the start of a new business can make a critical difference in a successful launch. Keep in mind that in order to get these types of incentives you will normally be expected to sign a lease for a minimum of three years. Always ask for free or reduced rent in the beginning to help offset the cost of move in and setup.

- Competitor Clauses

Competitor clauses are generally not offered to potential tenants that don't have knowledge of them; this type of incentive usually must be asked for. Several businesses close each year because of competition. There is nothing wrong with a business having competition or competitors but when you're choosing a location for your business, you must take steps to ensure that your landlord will not invite your competitors to become your neighbors. Keep in mind that once you sign on the dotted line, you are obligated to pay your landlord each month. So take necessary steps to ensure that this will be easy for you by asking for a Competitor's Clause to be included in your lease. This type of clause simply states that as long as you are leasing from a particular center, the center will not lease to another business that could adversely affect your ability to be profitable.

For example, if you're opening an ice cream shop in a center that holds 50 tenants, you would ask for a guarantee in writing that the center will not lease to a another ice cream shop. You can't do anything about a competitor opening up across the street from you, but you can make sure they don't open up in the same center as you. Remember, after you sign a lease, you are obligated to pay, and your landlord will expect payment even if they allow competition to open up next door. You must protect yourself by asking for a Competitor's Clause to be included in your lease. When considering a center for lease, be sure to ask whether or not you are allowed to include a Competitor's Clause. If the answer is no, then that might not be the center for you.

Chapter 9 Check List
Leasing Incentives

☐ Ask for free or reduced rent at the beginning of the lease to help offset startup costs.

☐ Ask if the landlord is willing to pay for or contribute toward the build out costs of your space. (See Chapter 10)

☐ Ask for a Competitor's Clause to be included in your lease.

Chapter 10
Build Out

Sometimes in choosing a commercial location, interior construction (sometimes referred to as build-out) is needed so that the space can meet your business functional needs. A great way to avoid a build-out is to choose a space that was previously used by another business. This will save you time and money because the construction is already done. However, if changes need to be made, here are a few things to ask and a few things to keep in mind:

- Will the landlord build the space out or will it be your responsibility?

- In some cases, the landlord will pay for interior construction as an incentive for you to lease from them.

- If the landlord will not be handling interior construction, you must find out if he or she requires that you use a certain construction company or contractor to do the work.

- You also should know whether or not the workers you use are required to be a part of a workers union. This will have an effect on the amount of hours that are worked each day and the time of completion of your construction project.

- You must also be clear about whether or not there are city or county requirements for the type of work that will be done; this includes drawings or sketches and permits. Know who is responsible for getting permits from local authorities.

- If the space needs to be built out, always ask for an estimated time of completion and then add at least four weeks. Construction projects are rarely finished on time; you don't want to lose credibility with your customers before getting started because you set an opening date that has to be pushed back.

Chapter 10 Check List
Build Out

☐ Ask if the landlord is willing to pay for or contribute toward the build-out costs of your space.

☐ If the interior construction of the space will be your responsibility, ask if you are required to use a certain construction company or contractor for the desired work and know whether or not the workers you use are required to be a part of a workers union.

☐ Be clear about whether or not there are city or county requirements for the type of work that will be done; including drawings, sketches, or permits. Know who is responsible for getting permits from local authorities.

☐ Ask for an estimated time of completion and then add at least four weeks.

Chapter 11
Maintenance

- Heating and Air-conditioning

Unless in a mall location, most commercial leases will require that the tenant be responsible for the maintenance of heating and air-conditioning units. In some cases, the landlord will require the tenant to have a maintenance contract with a licensed heating and air company. This is normally for the purpose of making sure all air filters are in good condition, units are working properly, and air ducts are clean and maintained. This expense should be calculated into your cost of leasing. If this requirement applies to your lease, you should do careful research into the terms of the maintenance contract and the customer reviews of your chosen company. Some landlords will require that you choose from a particular group of service providers. Make sure you are clear about what is and what is not covered under your service contract.

- Pest Control

Another area of maintenance to be considered is pest-control. A service contract may or may not be required for this service in your lease, particularly, if you are not a restaurant. Remember, it is not a good idea to assume - always ask BEFORE signing a lease.

Maintenance

☐ If you are purchasing a location, be sure all heating and air equipment is inspected and ask for a service record to be sure that all equipment was properly maintained.

☐ When leasing, find out if a maintenance contract with a licensed heating and air company is required.

☐ Make sure that the landlord has had all heating and air-conditioning units serviced and that they are in working order before moving in.

☐ Inquire as to whether or not the pest-control agreement will be a requirement of your lease. Ask if a certain company must be used.

Chapter 12
CAM

Most people that have never signed a commercial lease are unaware that most landlords charge for CAM. CAM stands for Common Area Maintenance. It is a charge that most tenants are required to pay for the maintenance and upkeep of common areas in shopping centers and strip malls. CAM charges normally cover things such as landscaping, outdoor lighting, trash pickup, and outdoor window cleaning. It is important to note that this charge is normally set by the landlord. As a tenant, you, as well as other tenants, are expected to pay your share of it while leasing in the center.

Keep in mind that the more upscale the center, the more expensive CAM charges will be. If you desire to have your business located in a center where customers walk past waterfalls and beds of roses on paved stone while listening to classical music, you will be expected to help pay for it. Most centers that are worth moving into will charge CAM. When inquiring about a location always asks if there is a CAM charge and if so, how much. You must know this in order to establish an accurate budget. Remember, it is your responsibility to do your due diligence.

Should you choose to locate your business in a center that charges CAM, it is very important that you always negotiate a set CAM rate. Unlike rent, CAM charges normally will not be capped in a written agreement unless you ask for it. If the cost of maintaining common areas goes up for the landlord, the increased cost can be passed on to the tenants without warning or limit unless agreed upon in writing. So it is very important to negotiate a set or capped CAM rate; this is an agreement between you and the landlord stating that CAM will never go above a certain amount or percentage during the term of your lease.

There was a consignment shop owner that had a very successful business located in a themed shopping center until the center was sold to a new owner. Upon taking ownership, the new owner decided he wanted to make more money from each tenant. Because the tenants were in legally binding leases, the new owner could not raise their rent simply because he wanted to. So what did he do? Because they never negotiated set percentages or prices for CAM, he raised the CAM rates for each tenant. This caused the tenants monthly rent to double - destroying their monthly budgets and profits in the process.

It is reasonable to think that over the course of a lease, common area maintenance charges will go up. However, it is important to protect yourself against astronomical rises in costs that are designed to line the pockets of the landlord's friends or relatives. No doubt when these charges were raised, in this particular center, the person that was being paid to maintain the center, most likely shared the same address or last name as the landlord. Remember, always negotiate a set or capped CAM rate.

Chapter 12 Check List
CAM

☐ Ask if your lease will require you to pay CAM charges and if so, how much.

☐ Know exactly what CAM charges will cover. Make a list of the services that will be provided as a result of CAM charges.

☐ Find out if CAM will be charged as a set rate or as a percentage of the space you plan to lease.

☐ Negotiate a capped CAM rate that will not exceed a certain amount or a certain percentage during the term of your lease.

Chapter 13
Utilities

It is important for you to know whether or not utilities are included in the amount you will pay for your space each month. It is very rare, but some landlords will include utility costs in the monthly rent. When utilities are not included and if the building is not totally electric, there are three services that you must think about; electric, water, and gas. In some cases, trash pickup will be considered a utility. If utilities are not included in your lease, it is important to understand that their cost will affect your overall budget. It is also important to know the average cost of utilities so that you can accurately calculate budget projections.

Average utility costs can be estimated in three ways. First, if the space has been leased before, you could simply ask the landlord about average costs. Second, if your space is similar in size to other tenants whose hours of operation mirror your future hours of operation, you could ask current tenants what their average monthly cost are. Third, you could ask the utility companies themselves. Here is a list of questions you want to ask the landlord and utility service providers:

- Am I required to pay a deposit in order to start service?
- How long will it take for service to begin at my business location after service has been requested?
- When are the due dates?
- Do I have a choice of service providers? Who are the service providers for my area?
- Do I have to sign a written contract for any of the services that will be needed?

- Does my particular location need to have a meter installed?
- Will I be on a shared meter with other tenants?

Again, you never want to assume - know the answer to these questions BEFORE signing a lease.

Chapter 13 Check List
Utilities

☐ Ask if utilities will be included in your monthly payments.

☐ Ask the landlord or other tenants with spaces that are the same size as yours about the average cost of utilities.

☐ Find out which utility companies service the location.

☐ Find out if a contract will have to be signed for any of the needed services.

☐ Ask whether or not a deposit will be required to start service at the location. Keep in mind that if required, the amount of the deposit will sometimes depend on the results of a credit check.

☐ Find out how long it will take for service to begin after it has been requested.

☐ Find out the due dates for each service that will be needed and note the due dates for accounting purposes.

☐ Find out if your location will need to have a meter installed before services can begin.

☐ Find out if you will be on a shared meter with any other tenants.

Chapter 14
Insurance

Most people know that businesses are required to carry some form of general liability insurance at all times. However, what is not known to many new business owners is that in most cases, your landlord will require that you provide them with coverage on your insurance policy as well. Coverage for yourself, your business, and the landlord is relatively inexpensive when you consider the possibilities of an incident occurring without insurance. Keep in mind that most retail centers will require that you carry a general liability insurance policy of at least $1 million. Policies are generally low in cost but may vary based on your specific industry or business.

Other forms of insurance that you may want to have are theft, fire, and property damage. Remember to always get quotes (never sign up with the first agent you talk to). To maximize your coverage, you may want to choose an insurance company that is known for ensuring businesses in your specific field.

Chapter 14 Check List
Insurance

☐ Ask if your landlord will require coverage on your insurance policy and know the coverage amount.

☐ Know the specific coverage that will be needed in order to receive accurate quotes.

☐ Receive quotes for coverage from multiple insurance companies for the best price.

☐ Research insurance companies that are known for covering businesses in your specific field.

Chapter 15
Create A Budget

As mentioned in "StartUp Easy Guide" - Volume 1, a budget should always be a part of your business plan. Creating a budget for your business is a great way to know how much your business will need to generate in order to be profitable. If you know how much your business will need to make in order to be profitable and how much your potential business may make, then you can make wise decisions about how much you should spend each month for a business location. Remember, income does not equal profit; income minus expenses equals profit.

You have not made a profit until ALL expenses related to doing business have been paid. Your budget should not be made to fit the location you choose; you should choose a location that fits your budget. The goal is to make a profit for yourself, not just for your landlord.

Chapter 15 Check List

Create A Budget

☐ Create a startup budget using the projected expenses of opening at the potential location.

☐ Create a monthly income and expenses budget using the projected monthly expenses of the potential location.

Chapter 16
Have A Business Plan

Most lending institutions require that a business plan be submitted when applying for a business loan. And in some cases, you will be required to present your business plan to potential landlords. If you are entering into a lease that is loaded with incentives, some landlords are going to want some type of assurance that you have a plan for success. It is a good idea to have a business plan ready and available in the form of a template that can be changed to reflect the cost of rent for any location you choose. This plan should include a budget with profit projections, as well as, a plan to market and advertise your new business in order to gain new customers.

The US government provides free assistance in creating a business plan through the Small Business Administration. Again, this will not be a requirement for all landlords but it is important that you be prepared and know where to receive help if it is needed.

Chapter 16 Check List
Have A Business Plan

☐ Create a business plan that can be customized to fit any location with a budget that can be customized for the expenses of any potential location.

Chapter 17
Personal Guarantees

Before choosing a certain center and signing a lease, you should know whether or not you will be required to sign a personal guarantee. In some cases, personal guarantees are asked for when the business that desires to lease is fairly new and has no credit history. It is important to know exactly what you're getting yourself into when signing a personal guarantee; signing a personal guarantee essentially means that you are promising to pay all rent owed under the terms of the lease whether your business succeeds or not. It means that should your business fail and close its doors, you are still responsible for any debt associated with the lease and that short of filing bankruptcy, it must be paid back by you. Understand that if you sign a personal guarantee on behalf of your business, you are in effect, removing yourself from the protections of incorporating where the lease is concerned.

Signing a personal guarantee means that if your business were to fail and if you failed to pay the remainder of the lease, the landlord has the right to sue you and come after your personal assets. Keep in mind that everything is negotiable and if you are not comfortable signing a personal guarantee, it should be expressed during the negotiation period. Depending upon how strongly you feel about this, you must also be willing to walk away from that particular center and be willing to locate somewhere else. It is important to note that not all landlords require personal guarantees. Many centers will allow you to use the credit of the business alone, even if the business is brand-new.

Chapter 17 Check List
Personal Guarantees

☐ Determine whether you are willing to sign a personal guarantee to secure a location.

☐ Find out if a personal guarantee is required to secure the location.

☐ If you're uncomfortable signing a personal guarantee, find out if the landlord will allow the lease to stand on the business credit alone.

Chapter 18
CO's and Fire Safety

When considering a location for your business, it is very important that you research and know local government requirements for fire safety. Fire safety requirements will vary depending upon the type of business that you're planning to open and the location. For example, most daycares are required to have working sprinkler systems and hooded vent systems for the stoves that will be used in food preparation. If a potential day care owner is considering centers or locations that don't have sprinkler systems in place, they are wasting their time. The safety requirements for a jewelry store will be vastly different from the safety requirements of a restaurant. It is up to you to know what your state and local government will require for the type of business you're opening.

Knowing these requirements will allow you to quickly eliminate locations that won't work for your type of business, while quickly identifying locations that will. Here are a few things that you should be aware of:

- **CO (Certificate of Occupancy)**

CO stands for Certificate of Occupancy. Most cities and counties will require that you have a CO for your location. The responsibility of issuing a CO to your business location normally falls to the city or county's fire department. If your location requires interior construction, a local building inspector may need to approve it as well.

Obtaining a CO will also require that your business have and maintain working fire extinguishers. The number of extinguishers needed is often based on the size of your space and the type of business you're opening. Each year, extinguishers must be serviced and will be inspected along with your exit lights by your local fire department. Having extinguishers serviced is very inexpensive but should be factored into your annual budget.

Depending upon your type of business and the amount of space your business will occupy, your location may also be required to have a certain number of restrooms, as well as, panic bars on the exit doors before a CO is issued. You must know the safety requirements before choosing a location in order to keep the costs of compliance to a minimum. Doing research before signing a lease can and will save you valuable time and money.

- **Maximum Occupancy**

At the time your business is issued a CO you will be told the maximum occupancy of your business location. Maximum occupancy is the number of people that your business is allowed to have in your location at any one time. For example, if you are opening a restaurant and your certificate of occupancy states that your maximum occupancy is 150 persons, then that is the total amount of employees and customers you are allowed to have in your restaurant at any one time. Businesses are normally required to openly display this number for the safety of their customers. Often concert venues, nightclubs, bars, and other places of large gatherings are monitored closely by authorities to be sure that their maximum occupancy is never exceeded.

Chapter 18 Check List
CO's and Fire Safety

☐ Know local government requirements for fire safety.

☐ Find out if there are specific regulations for your type of business.

☐ Find out if the potential location is equipped with the correct exit doors and has an adequate number of restrooms for a fast CO process.

☐ Find out if the potential maximum occupancy for the space matches your business needs.

Chapter 19
Signage

When choosing a location for your business is very important to know what type of sign your business will be required to install. The cost of signage can range from hundreds of dollars to thousands of dollars depending upon the type of signage that is desired or needed. Most centers and cities desire that local businesses have signage that is uniform in appearance and size. If you are located in an upscale shopping center, you should expect to pay more for signage than a business located in an industrial area or commercially zoned residential home. While researching potential locations, be sure to know the type of signage required at your location so that it can be factored into your startup costs.

Remember, whether you are installing a box sign or lettered sign, you should never except the first quote that you are given. Competition drives down costs. Always ask for a quote that includes installation. Often times, sign companies will quote the cost of the sign and the cost of installation separately. You must be sure that you understand what your total expenses will be.

In addition to this, be sure to discuss and know who will be responsible for obtaining a sign permit and submitting renderings to the local authorities for approval. Also, most times, the landlord will want to approve the size and color of your sign as well. The goal of the landlord will be for all tenant signs to maintain a uniform look. As with all projects that could affect your grand opening date, you should always ask your chosen sign company for an estimated time of completion.

Chapter 19 Check List
Signage

☐ Find out what type of sign your business will be required to install.

☐ Obtain quotes for the best prices.

☐ Find out if you or the sign company will be responsible for obtaining a sign permit.

☐ Find out if your sign will need to be submitted for approval by your landlord.

☐ Ask for an estimated time of completion and add time to be sure that there are no delays in your opening.

Works Citied

wikipedia.org

http://legal-dictionary.thefreedictionary.com

http://www.thefreedictionary.com